I0014469

CompTIA Linux+

Linux Certification Guide (LX0-103 & LX0-104exams)

By Erwin Haas

Copyright©2016 by Erwin Haas

All Rights Reserved

Copyright © 2016 by Erwin Haas

All rights reserved. No part of this publication may be reproduced, distributed, or transmitted in any form or by any means, including photocopying, recording, or other electronic or mechanical methods, without the prior written permission of the author, except in the case of brief quotations embodied in critical reviews and certain other noncommercial uses permitted by copyright law.

Table of Contents

Disclaimer

While all attempts have been made to verify the information provided in this book, the author does assume any responsibility for errors, omissions, or contrary interpretations of the subject matter contained within. The information provided in this book is for educational and entertainment purposes only. The reader is responsible for his or her own actions and the author does not accept any responsibilities for any liabilities or damages, real or perceived, resulting from the use of this information.

The trademarks that are used are without any consent, and the publication of the trademark is without permission or backing by the trademark owner. All trademarks and brands within this book are for clarifying purposes only and are the owned by the owners themselves, not affiliated with this document.

Introduction

The CompTIA Linux+ LX0-103 & LX0-104 exam emphasizes a number of topics. It is good for you to learn the details which are tested in these topics as most of them are wide. If you study the topics which are highly tested in the exam, then you will definitely pass it. The process of installation of Linux is highly tested, so you have to learn more about the various forms of installation media in Linux. Security is equally tested, so it is good for you to learn the various measures which can be taken to ensure that your Linux system is secure. This book is a guide on how to pass the CompTIA Linux+ LX0-103 & LX0-104 exams. Enjoy reading!

Chapter 1- Installation

Linux can be installed using a variety of media. Each of these installation media is associated with its own advantages and disadvantages, and this is all determined by the environment you are using. The various forms of installation media for Linux are discussed below:

1. Boot disk- this is also known as a boot floppy, and by itself, it cannot be referred to be an installation technique. The boot disk is used for launching the setup by use of the other forms of installation media. The disks are available in the form of floppy images on a CD-ROM, together with good software for copying these onto your floppies.

2. CD-ROM- this type of installation is very popular. For this to be used, you must have a system with the capability to boot from a CD-ROM. The Linux distribution which you need to install should also be made available on the CD. When you have that, you are just expected to insert the disk into the computer and then start it. The setup will definitely start automatically. However, some systems do not support booting up from the CD-ROM. In such a scenario, you

can use a Linux boot setup disk so as to launch the system.

There are various other forms of installation in Linux. Examples of these include Http, NFS, FTP, and SMB, and most of these in production areas for setting up workstations and servers. The reason why these methods are not common is that they are based on a network, meaning that one must have a working network so as to take advantage of them.

Installation Modes

Originally, the process of installing Linux only involved a small group of users. Some of the Linux distributions are now easy to install when compared to other commercial operating systems.

After launching the setup, you will be asked whether you need to install the distribution in "simple" mode or "advanced-expert" mode. In simple terms, you are just being asked whether you need to use the "text" mode or the "graphical" user interface (GUI). The use of a GUI is very simple and straightforward, as it is just a wizard which features menus of type, point, and click. The text mode is very harsh, is created for Linux geeks, and it will give one a very flexible installation process.

Despite the kind of mode that you need to use, it is good for you to adhere to the installation instructions provided by the distribution you are to use.

Installation of Linux Boot Loaders

Besides the partitions and their contents, the hard disks contain much. The MBR (master boot record) is the one responsible for holding the boot loader (or the boot manager) and the MBR partition table. The BIOS usually reads the boot loader and then executes it once the system has started to load. The boot loader then executes the Linux kernel into the memory and gets it running. This means that a hard disk is never configured completely unless the boot loader has been correctly configured.

LILO

This was the default boot loader in the Linux x86 architecture. The use of LILO as the boot loader has been replaced by GRUB< and for you to use LILO, you must install it in your hard disk and then configure your system to use it as the boot loader.

A typical LILO configuration should be as shown below:

```
# lilo.conf
#
# Global Options:
#
boot=/dev/hda
prompt
timeout=150
default=fedora
lba32
vga=normal
root=/dev/hda5
read-only
#
```

```
# Kernel Options (may have multiple):
#
image=/boot/vmlinuz-2.6.25
label=fedora
initrd=/boot/initrd-2.6.25
append="mem=2048M"
image=/boot/bzImage-2.6.26-experimental
label=debian
root=/dev/hda6
#
# Other Operating Systems Options (may have
multiple):
#
other=/dev/hda2
label=dos
```

Note that the defaults can be modified so as to meet what you need.

GRUB

This has many features compared to LILO, and this is why it has taken over as the default boot loader in most Linux distributions. Once you have edited the configuration options for Grub, there will be no need for you to reinstall it, and you will have many interactive options during the process of booting.

Grub is located at "/boot/grub/menu" by default. In some distributions such as Red Hat, Fedora, and Gentoo, the configuration file used is *"grub.config"* rather than the "menu.lst." This tool is capable of reading its configuration file during the boot process, and this is why you don't have to make any change to the configuration file.

Consider the sample GRUB configuration file given below:

 # grub.conf/menu.lst
#
 # Global Options:
#
default=0
timeout=15
splashimage=/grub/bootimage.xpm.gz
#

```
# Kernel Image Options:
#
title Fedora (2.6.25)
root (hd0,0)
kernel /vmlinuz-2.6.25 ro root=/dev/hda5
mem=2048M

initrd /initrd-2.6.25
title Debian (2.6.26-experimental)
root (hd0,0)
kernel (hd0,0)/bzImage-2.6.26-experimental ro
root=/dev/hda6

#
# Other operating systems
#
title DOS
rootnoverify (hd0,1)
chainloader +1
```

The Boot Process in Linux

A computer takes the following steps to load the operating system when booting:

1. The system is powered, and the CPU is made to look at a specified address to find a code stored there and then execute it. This is where the BIOS resides, so the CPU will have executed it.

2. The code for BIOS will then perform a number of tasks. Examples include checking for the hardware, configuring the hardware, and then looking for the boot sector. The boot loader is stored in the boot sector.

3. The boot loader will then take over from the BIOS. If you have a multi-staged loader, it will have to look for a secondary loader. Some of the boot loaders will directly go to the secondary loader in the active partition of the hard drive. With boot loaders such as Grub and LILO, you can do much.

4. The boot loader should now be geared towards getting the kernel, which is the final step. This is usually loaded into the computer memory and then executed.

5. The Linux kernel then takes over, and it performs tasks such initialization for devices, mounting of the root partition, and loading and execution of the initial program of this system. This system is usually set to "/sbin/init" by default.

6. The initial program will then get a process ID since it is the one to be executed on the system.

RunLevels in Linux

In Linux, runlevels are used to determine the features which are made available to the user. They range from 0 to 6, and each of these runlevels is assigned a set of services which will be made active. Once you boot up your Linux system, it enters into a particular runlevel, which you can specify. The following is a discussion of the purpose of each runlevel in Linux:

- 0- This changes the system from one state to another, and it typically shuts down the system.

- 1, s, or S- this specifies the single-user mode. The services started at this level will be determined by the Linux distribution you are using. It is normally used for low-level system maintenance operations such as resizing of the available partitions.

- \2- when in Debian and its related distributions, you get a multi-user mode with a graphical login. This run level has been left undefined in some of the Linux distributions.
- 3- on Red hat, Fedora, Mandriva, and some other distributions, you get a multi-user mode together and a console login screen.

- 4- this is left undefined by default, and is normally used for making some customizations.

- 5- on Red Hat, Fedora, Mandriva, and some other distributions, this has the same behavior as runlevel 3, but it has an X run and an XDM login.

- 6- this is for the purpose of rebooting the system. The system shuts down and then starts again, meaning that it is a transitional runlevel.

Chapter 2- Linux Command Line Tools

Shell Environment Variables

The environment is created in the form of strings which represent some key-value pairs. If you need to pass multiple values, you have to separate them using a colon (:). The pairs look as shown below:

KEY=value1:value2:...

For variables with significant white space, then you have to use double quotes.

KEY="value having spaces"

The variables in our case are the keys. The variables can either be environment variables or shell variables.

Environment variables are defined for the current shell, and these can be inherited by any of the child shells or processes.

We use them to pass information to processes which have been spawned from the shell.

Shell variables- these variables are contained exclusively in the shell where they have been set or defined.

How to Print the Variables

Each session in shell will keep its own shell and environment variables. There are a number of ways to access these. The commands "env" or "printenv" can be used for the purpose of printing the available environment variables in our system.

When in their default state, they should work in the same way. Execute the following command:

printenv

Which should give you the following output:

SHELL=/bin/bash

TERM=xterm

USER=demouser

LS_COLORS=rs=0:di=01;34:ln=01;36:mh=00:pi=40;
33:so=01;35:do=01;35:bd=40;33;01:cd=40;33;01:or=
40;31;01:su=37;41:sg=30;43:ca:...

MAIL=/var/mail/nicohsam

PATH=/usr/local/bin:/usr/bin:/bin:/usr/local/games
:/usr/games

PWD=/home/nicohsam

LANG=en_US.UTF-8

SHLVL=1

HOME=/home/nicohsam

LOGNAME=nicohsam

LESSOPEN=| /usr/bin/lesspipe %s

LESSCLOSE=/usr/bin/lesspipe %s %s

_=/usr/bin/printenv

There is a small difference between the two commands. With the "*printenv*" command, you can request to have the specific value for a particular variable. Consider the example given below:

printenv SHELL

With the *"env"* command, you can modify the environment which programs run just by passing the variable definitions within the command. Consider the example given below:

env VAR1="yourvariable" command_run command_options

The following are some of the common environment variables:

- SHELL- this is used for describing the shell which will interpret the commands which you type in.

- TERM- this is used for describing the type of terminal which is to be emulated when you are running the shell.

- USER- this represents the user who has been logged in currently.

- PWD- this represents the directory which is currently running.

- OLDPWD- this is the old working directory.

- LS_COLORS- this is used for representing the color codes which will be used for adding some colored output to our "ls" command.

- MAIL- this is the path to the mailbox of the current user.

- HOME- the home directory for the current user.

- _: this is the command which has been executed most previously.

Getting Help

There are a number of ways how to get help on a specific command on Linux.

If you are not sure about how a specific command should be used, just type the command and then add "-h" or "-help.. If you don't know the usage of the "wget" command, type the following:

wget –help or wget –h

The command will give too much information. That is why you should pipe it to less as shown below:

wget –help | less

```
GNU Wget 1.17.1, a non-interactive network retriever.
Usage: wget [OPTION]... [URL]...

Mandatory arguments to long options are mandatory for short options too.

Startup:
  -V,  --version                display the version of Wget and exit
  -h,  --help                   print this help
  -b,  --background             go to background after startup
  -e,  --execute=COMMAND        execute a '.wgetrc'-style command

Logging and input file:
  -o,  --output-file=FILE       log messages to FILE
  -a,  --append-output=FILE     append messages to FILE
  -d,  --debug                  print lots of debugging information
  -q,  --quiet                  quiet (no output)
  -v,  --verbose                be verbose (this is the default)
  -nv, --no-verbose             turn off verboseness, without being quiet
       --report-speed=TYPE      output bandwidth as TYPE.  TYPE can be bits
  -i,  --input-file=FILE        download URLs found in local or external FILE
  -F,  --force-html             treat input file as HTML
  -B,  --base=URL               resolves HTML input-file links (-i -F)
                                  relative to URL
       --config=FILE            specify config file to use
       --no-config              do not read any config file
       --rejected-log=FILE      log reasons for URL rejection to FILE

Download:
  -t,  --tries=NUMBER           set number of retries to NUMBER (0 unlimits)
:
```

The output can also be piped through grep if you need to know more than a specific option. Consider the command given below:

wget –help | grep proxy

This gives the following output:

```
bash-4.3$ wget --help | grep proxy
       --no-proxy                    explicitly turn off proxy
       --proxy-user=USER             set USER as proxy username
       --proxy-password=PASS         set PASS as proxy password
bash-4.3$ 
```

Tab Completion

Tab completion can help you if you are not sure about how to write a certain command, or a certain file name. Suppose you have a command which starts with "gnome-session" but you don't have the rest, you can open the terminal, type "gnome-session" and then hit the tab key twice. A number of options will be presented to you. From the options, just select the one that you want.

Man

This command is used for showing many details regarding a Linux command. If you need to see the man pages for the "wget" command, you will just have to execute the command "man wget."

Info

Some commands in Linux do not have man pages, but instead, we use the "info" command to view details regarding them. An example of such a command is the "tar" command which is used for backup and recovery in Linux.

Instead of typing "man tar," you use "info tar." This will provide many details regarding the command.

Apropos

This is used for searching the man pages which have a certain phrase. We just need to search for a command which can help us to do something. The command is the same to the "man –k" command.

Whatis

This command will give you a summary of a particular command in one line, and the summary is usually taken from the man pages of the command. If you need to have a quick preview of the function of a specific command, use "whatis."

Chapter 3- Management RPM

Most Linux distributions use packages to group their software to get a RPM package manager (RPM). Although this system was initially made for Red Hat, it has been changed to support other forms of Linux distributions.

RPM packaging works by packaging metadata together with the software for the application. The metadata can be version numbers, files contained in the package, package description, information regarding the packager, and several other items. Dependencies and scripts can also be featured in the metadata.

The *"rpm"* command was previously used for the purpose of installing and managing the RPM packages. However, most of the uses of this command have been taken over by the *"yum"* command. Graphical tools have also been introduced, and these can be used for the purpose of installation and management of the RPM packages.

INVESTIGATING RPM PACKAGES

It is good for you to get an RPM package and then investigate it. If you have Red Hat installed, you can follow the steps given below:

1. Download a package- if your Red Hat system has been registered with the Red Hat network, get the package using the command "yumdownloader," As an example, you can run the following command from the shell, but do it as the root:

   # yumdownloader amanda-2*

2. Use a RHEL installation DVD- if you have this DVD, just insert into your computer and then wait for the mounting to take place automatically. You can then start the shell and change the directory which is currently on the CD.

USING THE RPM COMMAND

Once you have downloaded the package in the local directory, there are a number of ways to investigate the package before going ahead to install it. The yum good is good when it comes to installation and removal of a package, but the "*rpm*" is the best when it comes to querying and validating of a package.

The query package is implemented using the "*-q*" option on the "*rpm*" command, and you have to indicate what you need to query. If you need to query a particular package before having to install it, you can add the "*-p*" option along with the name of the package as the argument.

If you need to view information regarding the Amanda package which is located in the current directory, you can include the option "*-i*" to the command "rpm —qp" as shown below:

 # rpm -qpi amanda-2.6.1p2-7.el6.x86_64.rpm

Once you have learned the purpose for a file, you may need to know more about the files which it has. The "*-l*" option can be used for listing the files contained in the package as shown below:

```
# rpm -qpl amanda-2.6.1p2-7.el6.x86_64.rpm
/etc/amanda
/etc/amanda/DSet2
/etc/xinetd.d/amanda
/usr/lib64/amanda
/usr/lib64/amanda/amanda-sh-lib.sh
/usr/lib64/amanda/chg-glue
```

Note that the listing of the files has been shortened so that space can be saved. A full output from the command will show that the package has configuration files, documentation, and scripts used with Amanda. The configuration files contained in the Amanda package can be listed as follows:

```
# rpm -qpc amanda-2.6.1p2-7.el6.x86_64.rpm
/etc/xinetd.d/amanda
/var/lib/amanda/.amandahosts
```

The documentation in the Amanda package can be shown as follows:

```
# rpm -qpd amanda-2.6.1p2-7.el6.x86_64.rpm
/usr/share/doc/amanda-2.6.1p2/COPYRIGHT
/usr/share/doc/amanda-2.6.1p2/NEWS |
/usr/share/doc/amanda-2.6.1p2/README
/usr/share/doc/amanda-2.6.1p2/README-rpm
```

/usr/share/man/man5/amanda-archive-format.5.gz

/usr/share/man/man5/amanda.conf.5.gz

/usr/share/man/man7/amanda-auth.7.gz

/usr/share/man/man7/amanda-scripts.7.gz

/usr/share/man/man8/amarchiver.8.gz

/usr/share/man/man8/amrestore.8.gz

The bug fixes and changes which are associated with the package can be shown as follows:

 # rpm -qp --changelog amanda-2.6.1p2-7.el6.x86_64.rpm

* Fri May 06 2016 John George <jgeorge@redhat.com> 2.6.1p2-7

- added amoldrecover description to amrecover man page

- Resolves: #593775

* Sat May 07 2016 John George <jgeorge@redhat.com> 2.6.1p2-6

- removed non existing -k option from amfetchdump help

- Resolves: #596050

You can also make use of the *"rpm"* command to check on whether the package is okay, but not corrupted. This is possible since the package has been signed, and it can be checked alongside a public key which has to be imported into the system.

Consider the command given below, which shows how an Amanda package can be validated:

 # rpm -qp --checksig amanda-2.6.1p2-7.el6.x86_64.rpm

amanda-2.6.1p2-7.el6.x86_64.rpm: rsa sha1 (md5) pgp md5 OK

From the output shown above, the package is okay, meaning that it was not corrupted at all. After modifying the package and running the command again, you should get an error as shown below:

 # rpm -qp --checksig amanda-2.6.1p2-7.el6.x86_64.rpm

amanda-2.6.1p2-7.el6.x86_64.rpm: rsa sha1 (MD5) PGP MD5 NOT OK

Managing Files and Directories

For you to be a pro in using the Linux terminal, you must be aware of the necessary commands for managing files and navigating through the directories.

If you need to find the directory that you are in in relation to the filesystem, you can make use of the "*pwd*" command. It will then show you the directory you are in:

Pwd

The home directory in Linux is named after the name of the account user. Suppose that the previous command gave me the following:

/home/nicohsam

The above output just means that the user "*nicohsam*" is logged into the system, and the directory "*/nicohsam*" is found in the "*/home*" directory, which is referred to as a top-level directory and is represented using a single slash "/."

Listing the contents of a directory

Since you have learned how to display your directory, it is good for you to know how to display the contents which it has. This is only done by use of the "ls" command, which means *"list."* Just type the command and press the enter key. This will list all the files contained in the directory:

```
bash-4.3$ ls
README.txt   me.c
bash-4.3$
```

In my case, I am using CentOS and I have two files in the directory, that is, *"README.txt"* and *"me.c."*

It is possible for you to add some flags to the command so as to override the default behavior. If you need to display all the contents, but in a long form, you can use the "-l" option as shown below:

ls –l

This gives the output shown below:

```
bash-4.3$ ls -l
total 4
-rw-r--r-- 1 20661 20661 978 May 10 05:39 README.txt
-rw-r--r-- 1 20661 20661   0 May 10 05:58 me.c
```

As shown in the output, we have plenty of information. The permissions have been specified, as well as the size and the date that the file was created.

In most directories, some files and subdirectories are hidden. The "-a" flag can be added to the "ls" command for you to view these.

```
bash-4.3$ ls -a
.  ..  .cg_conf  .viminfo  README.txt  me.c
```

As shown in the above output, we have two hidden files, alongside the special indicators in the form of "." and ".." As you might have noticed, configuration files are usually stored as hidden files in Linux. The dots are just methods which are mostly used for the purpose of referring to the related directories. The single dot is an indication of the current directory, while the double dot is an indication of the parent directory.

To change your current directory, you should use the "cd" command. The command should be followed by the name of the directory to change to.

If you need to move to the parent directory of your current directory, meaning that you are moving back up, you should use the two dots we discussed earlier.

Viewing Files

The "*less*" command is very good for one to view a file, and it is usually referred to as the "*pager*" since it allows one to view the contents of their file in pages. This command will run and keep on occupying the screen until that time when you exit it.

In your terminal, type the command "less /etc/services." With the command, the file /etc/services will be opened on the window, and only the section which fits in there.

```
# /etc/services:
#
# Network services, Internet style
# IANA services version: last updated 2015-04-10
#
# Note that it is presently the policy of IANA to assign a single well-known
# port number for both TCP and UDP; hence, most entries here have two entries
# even if the protocol doesn't support UDP operations.
# Updated from RFC 1700, ``Assigned Numbers'' (October 1994).  Not all ports
# are included, only the more common ones.
#
# The latest IANA port assignments can be gotten from
#       http://www.iana.org/assignments/port-numbers
# The Well Known Ports are those from 0 through 1023.
# The Registered Ports are those from 1024 through 49151
# The Dynamic and/or Private Ports are those from 49152 through 65535
#
# Each line describes one service, and is of the form:
#
# service-name  port/protocol  [aliases ...]   [# comment]

tcpmux          1/tcp                           # TCP port service multiplexer
tcpmux          1/udp                           # TCP port service multiplexer
rje             5/tcp                           # Remote Job Entry
rje             5/udp                           # Remote Job Entry
echo            7/tcp
echo            7/udp
discard         9/tcp           sink null
discard         9/udp           sink null
/etc/services
```

If you need to scroll through the file, use the up and down arrows on your keyboard. If you need to page down one whole screen, just press the space bar or the Page Down key, or hit "Ctrl - f" on your keyboard. If you need to return back, just hit the "Page Up" button or pres the shortcut "Ctrl –b."

If you need to search for some text inside the document, type a forward slash "/" followed by the name of the text. If you need to search for "protocol," type "/protocol." Once the first case is found, the search will stop, and for you to continue searching, you should type a lower case "n."

If you need to move back to the previous result, type upper case "N." To quit the program, just press "q."

Manipulating Files and Directories

The CompTIA Linux+ LX0-103 & LX0-104 exam usually covers the process of creation and manipulation of files and directories, so it will be good for you to learn more about it.

Creating a file using "touch"

There are many programs which can be used for creating files in Linux. The "touch" command is the most popular program for doing this. The command will create an empty file with the specified name and in the specified location.

We need to create a file with the name "*doc1*." Use the command given below:

touch doc1

To verify whether the file was created, use the "*ls*" command as shown below:

```
bash-4.3$ ls
README.txt   doc1   me.c
bash-4.3$ █
```

Yes, the file has been created as shown in the above output.

If the command is used on an existing file, it will update the data which is contained in the filesystem in terms of the time at which it was last accessed and modified.

It is possible for us to create multiple files at once. Absolute paths can also be used. If we are using the account "*nicohsam,*" we can do the following:

touch /home/nicohsam/doc2 /home/nocohsam/doc3

```
bash-4.3$ ls
README.txt   doc1   doc2   doc3   me.c
bash-4.3$
```

The files have then been created, as shown in the above output.

The "mkdir" command

This command is used for the purpose of creating empty directories. Suppose that you need to create a directory with the name "*mydir.*" You can use the following command:

mkdir mydir

It is possible for us to create a directory within the previously created directory. Suppose we need to call it "*sample.*" The following command can be used for that purpose:

mkdir mydir/sample

It is also possible for us to work with nested directories in Linux. The "-p" option can be used for that purpose, and it will help us create the path for our directory. Consider the command given below:

mkdir -p my/other/dir

The command will work by first creating the directory "*my,*" and then it creates the directory "*other*" within the "*my*" directory. The directory named "*dir*" will then be created within the previous two directories.

The "mv" command

The "mv" command can be used for moving a file from one location to another. To move the file *"doc1"* to the directory "sample," we can use the following command:

mv doc1 sample

With the command, we just have to specify the files which we need to move and then the final location for the files. The file can be moved back to the home directory by use of the dot reference which will refer to our current directory. Ensure that you are in the home directory, and then execute the following command:

mv sample/doc1 .

The "mv" command is also used for the purpose of renaming both files and directories. If you need to change the name of the directory *"sample"* to *"sampling,"* use the following command:

mv sample sampling

The "cp" command

This command can be used for making a copy of an existing file or item. The doc3 can be moved to a new file with the name doc4 as shown below:

cp doc3 doc4

If we had used the "mv" command, the file doc3 would not exist now, but with the cp command, both doc3 and doc4 will exist, meaning that you have just made a duplicate of the file.

If you need to copy a directory, the flag "-r" must be used with the command. The flag represents a "recursive" copy, meaning the directory will be copied together with its contents. It has to be used even when the directory is empty.

If you need to copy "my" directory structure to the structure named "our," we will use the command given below:

cp -r my our

In files, if the target is found to exist, it is overwritten. However, with directories, if the target is found to exist, the directory will be copied into the target.

cp doc1 our

In the command, a new file with the name *"doc1"* will be created and then copied into the directory *"our."*

The "rm" and "rmdir" commands

For us to delete a file in Linux, we use the "rm" command. However, when using this command, you have to be extra careful as there is no reverse to it, meaning that you may end up destroying important files from your system.

If you need to remove a regular file, just pass it to the *"rm"* command and it will be deleted permanently. This is shown below:

rm doc1

The above command will delete the file "doc1" from your current directory.

To remove the directory "sample" contained within the "mydir" directory from the system, we can use the following command:

rmdir mydir/sample

To get rid of a non-empty directory, you will have to use the "*rm*" command once again. However, this has to be used together with the "-r" flag, which will remove the directory together with its contents recursively.

For you need to remove the "*our*" directory together with its contents, you should use the following command:

rm –r our

Again, note that the commands are permanent, so ensure that the command you type is the one which you need to execute.

Editing Files

At this point, you are aware of how to manipulate files as objects but not how to edit them and add content to the files.

You can use the nano editor for this purpose, as it is good for beginners. The command will however occupy the whole of the terminal during the time it is being used. The command can be used opening existing files or for creating new ones.

To open the file "*doc1*" for editing purposes, you can execute the following command:

nano doc1

The command will open the file. If you are in the editor and you need to get some help, just hit "CTRL-G." Once you are done with browsing the help, you can type "CTRL-X," and this will help you to get back to your document. You can then type the content which you need to add to your file, and this can be any text.

For you to type the content, you just have to type "CTRL-O." They will ask you to confirm the name of the file by which to save it, so you just have to type "Y" or "N" to discard the mad e changes and then exit, or "CTRL −C" so as to cancel the operation for exit.

It is possible for you to view the contents which you have added to your file. This can be done using either the "*cat*" or the "*less*" command. Once you open the file using less, remember to use the "q" to quit.

```
bash-4.3$ cat doc1
This is my first document in Linux
I enjoy using Linux. Thank you
```

You may also choose to use the vim or the vi editor. However, this is an advanced editor, and it needs to be used by experts.

We don't recommend that you use it unless you are a Linux
Geek.

Process Management

Management of processes is an important part of the
CompTIA A+ exam, and no exam will be set without some
questions on this topic.

Processes are used to refer to running applications in Linux.
This is why you should have a mechanism which will help you
manage these running applications. Let us discuss the aspects
of process management which are mostly tested in the
CompTIA Linux+ LX0-103 & LX0-104exam.

Viewing running processes

Top

This is a very simple command, and displays a list of all the
processes which are in a state of execution. You just have to
type the command on the terminal, as shown below:

top

```
top - 09:27:51 up 30 days,  2:10,  0 users,  load average: 9.17, 8.85, 9.24
Tasks:    4 total,    1 running,    3 sleeping,    0 stopped,    0 zombie
%Cpu(s):  8.0 us,   9.9 sy,   0.0 ni, 81.2 id,   0.9 wa,   0.0 hi,   0.1 si,   0.0 st
KiB Mem : 26386318+total, 12045908+free, 80418656 used, 62985432 buff/cache
KiB Swap:  8101884 total,  5853884 free,  2248000 used. 17080614+avail Mem

  PID USER      PR  NI    VIRT    RES    SHR S %CPU %MEM     TIME+ COMMAND
   39 23401     20   0   54872   2028   1504 R  0.3  0.0   0:00.06 top
    1 23401     20   0 1023900  78276   7388 S  0.0  0.0   0:02.47 --CODINGGROUND-
   25 23401     20   0   16136   1916   1536 S  0.0  0.0   0:00.01 sh
   31 23401     20   0   16132   1932   1548 S  0.0  0.0   0:00.01 bash
```

As shown in the figure representing output, the statistics about
the available processes have been shown. We have 1 process in
a running state, and 3 processes in a sleeping state. As shown,
in total, you have 4 processes. At the bottom, you can see the
processes which are running and the statistics associated with
them.

Htop

This command is an improved version of the "*top*" command,
and it has been made available in the repositories. You have to
begin by installing it from the command line, using the
command given below:

sudo apt-get install htop

Once you run the htop command, you get some output which
is more user friendly.

The "ps" command

The "top" and "htop" commands are not very flexible when it comes to viewing the running processes. When we call this command without arguments, we get some output which looks as follows:

```
bash-4.3$ ps
  PID TTY          TIME CMD
   25 pts/0    00:00:00 sh
   31 pts/0    00:00:00 bash
   46 pts/0    00:00:00 ps
bash-4.3$
```

As shown above, the shown processes are the ones associated with the current user and the terminal session.

If you need to get a comprehensive picture about the processes which are running, just run the command given below:

ps aux

The command just tells the ps to show us the processes which are owned by all users, and this is done in a user-friendly form. In my case, the command gives me the following output:

```
bash-4.3$ ps aux
USER          PID %CPU %MEM    VSZ    RSS TTY       STAT START   TIME
21872           1  0.8  0.0 1023900 77112 ?         Ssl  11:20   0:02
21872          25  0.0  0.0  16136  1916 pts/0      Ss   11:20   0:00
21872          31  0.0  0.0  16132  1896 pts/0      S    11:20   0:00
21872          33  0.0  0.0  50468  1808 pts/0      R+   11:24   0:00
```

The command just tells the "ps" to show the processes which are owned by all users in a friendly format. To see the processes in a tree form, whereby a hierarchy will be presented to you, you can execute the following command:

ps axjf

In my case, the command gives me the following as the output:

```
 PPID    PID   PGID   SID TTY      TPGID STAT    UID   TIME COMMAND
    0      1      1     1 ?           -1 Ssl   21872   0:02 --CODINGGROUND--
    1     25     25    25 pts/0       34 Ss    21872   0:00 sh
   25     31     31    25 pts/0       34 S     21872   0:00  \_ /bin/bash
   31     34     34    25 pts/0       34 R+    21872   0:00      \_ ps axjf
bash-4.3$
```

Process IDs

In both Unix-like systems and Linux, each process is identified by a process ID, or the PID. This is then used by the operating system for the purpose of identifying and keeping track of the available processes.

The *"pgrep"* command can provide us with an easy way of getting the PID of a process.

Since we have a process named *"bash"*running in our system, we can execute the following command to get its ID:

pgrep bash

```
bash-4.3$ pgrep bash
31
bash-4.3$
```

You have to note that the first process to be launched once the system has been started is given an ID of 1, and this can be viewed by executing the command *"pgrep init."* The process is responsible for the spawning of the other process contained in the system.

The parent for any process is the process which spawned it, and it is identified by a parent process id (PPID). In any case in which the parent process is killed, then the child process will die.

Sending Process Signals

The *"kill"* command provides us with an easy way to pass signals to a particular program in Linux. This command is mostly used for killing the process with the ID that you specify:

kill PID_of_process

The above command will send a signal to the process. The TERM signal will tell the process to end. The process will then perform any clean-up operations and then exit in a smooth manner.

Note that there is a number associated with each signal which can be passed in place of the name. As examples, use -9 instead of "kill" and -15 instead of "TERM."

Although you may think that signals are used for killing processes only, that is not the case. With several daemons, they usually restart once they a re given the hang-up or "HUP" signal. Apache is an example of such a program:

sudo kill -HUP apache_pid

When the above command is executed, Apache will have to reload the configuration file and then continue providing the service. If you need to see the list of signals which can be sent with kill, you just have to execute the following command:

kill –l

The commands give me the following output:

```
bash-4.3$ kill -l
 1) SIGHUP        2) SIGINT       3) SIGQUIT      4) SIGILL       5) SIGTRAP
 6) SIGABRT       7) SIGBUS       8) SIGFPE       9) SIGKILL     10) SIGUSR1
11) SIGSEGV      12) SIGUSR2     13) SIGPIPE     14) SIGALRM     15) SIGTERM
16) SIGSTKFLT    17) SIGCHLD     18) SIGCONT     19) SIGSTOP     20) SIGTSTP
21) SIGTTIN      22) SIGTTOU     23) SIGURG      24) SIGXCPU     25) SIGXFSZ
26) SIGVTALRM    27) SIGPROF     28) SIGWINCH    29) SIGIO       30) SIGPWR
31) SIGSYS       34) SIGRTMIN    35) SIGRTMIN+1  36) SIGRTMIN+2  37) SIGRTMIN+3
38) SIGRTMIN+4   39) SIGRTMIN+5  40) SIGRTMIN+6  41) SIGRTMIN+7  42) SIGRTMIN+8
43) SIGRTMIN+9   44) SIGRTMIN+10 45) SIGRTMIN+11 46) SIGRTMIN+12 47) SIGRTMIN+13
48) SIGRTMIN+14  49) SIGRTMIN+15 50) SIGRTMAX-14 51) SIGRTMAX-13 52) SIGRTMAX-12
53) SIGRTMAX-11  54) SIGRTMAX-10 55) SIGRTMAX-9  56) SIGRTMAX-8  57) SIGRTMAX-7
58) SIGRTMAX-6   59) SIGRTMAX-5  60) SIGRTMAX-4  61) SIGRTMAX-3  62) SIGRTMAX-2
63) SIGRTMAX-1   64) SIGRTMAX
bash-4.3$
```

Using Name to Send Process Signals

Although Linux geeks normally use the PIDs for sending signals to processes, the names can also be used for the same purpose. The "pkill" command functions in the same way as the "kill" command, with the only difference being that it works with the process name rather than the PID. The command given below shows how this can be used:

pkill -9 ping

The command can also be written as follows:

kill -9 `pgrep ping`

Sometimes, you may want to send a signal to each instance of a process contained in the system. The "killall" command can help you in doing this, as shown below:

killall firefox

Adjusting the Priorities for Processes

In a server environment, one is expected to make adjustments to the processes which are given priority. This is because some processes are critical for the system to be okay, while others can be executed if the resources remain.

A value named "niceness" is used for controlling priorities in Linux. Tasks with a higher priority are considered to be less nice, since they will not be sharing resources. Processes with a low priority are considered to be nice, since they will need to use a minimal amount of resources.

Once you run the "top" command on your system, you are presented with a column labeled "NI," and this represents the nice value for a process.

PID	USER	PR	NI	VIRT	RES	SHR	S	%CPU	%MEM	TIME+
27	22887	20	0	54872	2032	1504	R	0.3	0.0	0:00.05
1	22887	20	0	1023900	77096	7332	S	0.0	0.0	0:01.91
20	22887	20	0	16136	1916	1536	S	0.0	0.0	0:00.01
26	22887	20	0	16132	1896	1520	S	0.0	0.0	0:00.01

For the highest priority, anice value can range between "-19/-20," while for the lowest priority the nice value can range between "19/20." If you need to use the nice value for a process to execute it, do it as shown below:

nice -n 15 command_to_be_executed

This will only work when you are beginning a new program.

For you to alter the nice value of a program which is in existence, you can use a tool with the name "renice" as shown below:

renice 0 PID_to_prioritize

Chapter 4- Security

Managing File Permissions in Linux

Although Linux has a built-in security feature, managing file permissions is a good way that the security of a Linux system can be ensured.

Each file and directory in Linux has three permission groups:

- owner- these permissions are only applied to the owner of the file or directory, and the actions of the other users are not affected in any way.

- group- this permission will only apply to the group which has been assigned to the file or the directory, but the actions of the other users will not be affected.

- all users- this will be applied to all of the users in the system, and this has to be watched carefully.

Permission Types

Each file or directory in Linux is associated with three types of basic permissions which include the following:

1. read- this is the capability of the user to read the contents of your file.

2. write- this refers to the capability of the user to write to or modify the files in your system.

3. execute- this permission will affect the capability of a user to execute a file or view the contents in a particular directory.

The output from the command "ls –l" can tell us more about the available permissions on a file. Consider the permission given below:

_rwxrwxrwx 1 owner:group

The special character marked with an underscore is just a special permissions flag which can differ. The set of three characters (rwx) which follow specifies the owner permissions. The three sets of permissions which follow (rwx) signify the Group permissions. The rest of the three characters represent permissions for all users.

These are then fo9llowed by an integer character which represents the hardlinks to your file. The last part is for Owner:Group assignment.

Defining Permissions Explicitly

For permissions to be stated explicitly, one will have to reference both the permission type and the permission group. The following are the permission groups which are to be used:

- u - Owner

- g – Group

-

- o or a - All Users

When assigning permissions, we use – and + as the operators. This will signify to the system whether it should add or remove the various permissions. The permission types include the following:

- r – Read

- w – Write

- x – Execute

Suppose that you have a file named "*doc1*" whose permissions have been set to "*_rw_rw_rw,*" meaning that the owner, the group, and the other users have read and write permission on the file. Suppose that weneed to remove the write and read permissions from the users group.

For this to be done, we have to execute the command:

CHMOD A-RW DOC1

If we were to add the permission, we would have executed the following command:

chmod a+rw doc1

As shown in the demonstration, to add the permission, you just have to use a plus symbol rather than the minus symbol.

Binary permissions for Setting Permissions in Linux

For you to set permissions using binaries, you have to enter three characters. Consider the example given below:

chmod 640 doc1

The above command will mean that the owner will have read and write permissions, the group has read permissions, and there are no rights for the other users on the files.

The first permission is a representation of the Owner permissions, the second is a representation of the Group permissions, while the third number is a representation of permissions for the other users. The numbers are just representing the rwx string in a binary format.

- *r = 4*

- $w = 2$

- $x = 1$

What you do is that you add the numbers so that you can get the number representing the wanted permissions. Binary permissions will have to be added to each of three permission groups.

If you need to add a read permission to doc1, you will execute the command "***chmod 740 doc1.***"

Owners and Groups

It is possible for one to change the owner or the group which has been assigned to a file. For this to be done, we use the "chown" command. The command takes the syntax given below:

CHOWN OWNER:GROUP FILENAME

If you need to change the ownership of doc1 to user1 and then change the group to gamily, you would do it as follows:

CHOWN USER1:FAMILY DOC1

Firewalls

The firewall is the mechanism which checks on the traffic which is incoming and the traffic which is outgoing for security purposes. It protects unwanted traffic from getting into your network.

A firewall employs the following mechanisms so as to accomplish its tasks:

1. stealth mode

   This involves configuring the system in such a way that it will not respond to the ping requests. Ping requests are used for testing whether a system which has been connected to the network is up or not. It works by sending a data packet to the machine with a specified IP address, and then waits for a response. If the user gets a response, they will know that the IP address exists in the network. In this mode, the firewall is configured in such a way that it doesn't respond to ping requests. Attackers will only attack the hosts which respond to the ping requests. If you remain silent on the attacker ping requests, you will have remained anonymous, meaning that you will have a low chance of being attacked.

2. Blocking and Port Forwarding

Small systems and businesses will often use the mechanism of port blocking so as to protect themselves from attacks. In most cases, computer systems use ports for the purposes of communication. You can use a firewall to block ports which you need to stay open in your system. An example of this is the FTP (File Transfer Protocol) which makes use of port 21. If you do not need anyone to access your system via this port, you can block port 21 on your system.

Port forwarding is also an important mechanism for ensuring that your system is kept secure. Consider a situation in which you have two Linux systems within your network, and you need to configure one in such a way that you will be in a position to telnet into it once you are outside the network. In such a case, you will configure the firewall in such a way that it will forward traffic through port 21 to the host which you need to access remotely. When the firewall sees the traffic coming through port 21, it will forward it to the host with the IP address that you specified. If you have multiple systems within your system, it will be good for you to configure this.

3. Packet filtering

Packet filtering is a common mechanism for providing security to your Linux system but it is not available in home businesses and small systems. Data is usually transmitted in the form of packets, and each packet has a specification of its origin and destination. Firewalls employ the use of filtering rules so as to allow in or disallow packets. An example of this is when you allow ftp packets but disallow telnet. If you realize that a particular IP address is suspicious, you can block it from accessing the network.

Kernel Security

The kernel in Linux controls networking, thus, there is a need for us to keep it secure. The version of the kernel should be kept up to date so that we can stay protected from the latest network attacks. The following are some of the measures which can be employed to ensure that the Linux kernel has been secured:

1. Syn cookies-

   A SYN attack is a type of denial of service of attack in which your services are consumed and your computer is forced to restart. There is a great reason for you to enable syn cookies to protect yourself against these. The following command can be used for enabling this feature in 2.2.x kernel:

root# echo 1 > /proc/sys/net/ipv4/tcp_syncookies <P>

2. Firewalling
   This option is good if there is a need for a firewall to be configured in your machine, perform masquerading, or yearn to protect the dial-up workstation from anyone who tries to enter via a PPP dial-up interface.

3. Firewall packet logging

   This is a feature which will give you information regarding the packets that are received and sent from your own network.

4. Dropping source routed frames

   It is good for you to enable this feature in your system. Source routed frames will have the whole path to their destination in the packet. The routers through which your packet passes will not have to inspect it but just to forward it. With this, harmful data may enter into your system, and the security will have been breached.

5. Masquerading

   A computer in the local network secured by the Linux box may need to send some data to the outside network. In such a case, the box can be used to masquerade as the host, meaning that the traffic will be forwarded outside, but it will appear as if it originated from our firewall box. ICMP masquerading can also be used, in which case only the UDP and TCP traffic will masqueraded.

6. Packet signatures

This feature is available in the Linux kernel 2.2.x, and it provides a mechanism for signing NCP packets to implement a stringer security. It is possible for you to leave it disabled, but if you need to use it, take advantage and use it.

7. Firewall packet netlink device

With this feature, it is possible for you to analyze the first 128 bits you receive from your packets, and this will help you know whether it is valid or not, and take the necessary action such as forwarding or dropping the packet.

Using GPG

The GN U privacy Guard (GPG) is an implementation for public key cryptography. It ensures that there is a secure transmission of messages between the necessary parties and is good for verifying whether the origin of a message is genuine or not.

Public key encryption, which is the technique that GPG relies on, involves splitting of the stages of encryption and decryption of messages to get two stages.

The sender of the message has to sign it with their private key before sending the message. The recipient of the message will then use their public key to verify whether the message comes from a genuine source or not. With such a mechanism, it will be impossible for a third-party to spoof the identity of the sender and the message will have been kept secure. The message will be kept secure, as no corruption can be done to it during transmission.

Setting Up GPG Keys

If you are using Ubuntu 12.04, the GPG should come installed by default. If nit has not been installed, use the following command to install it:

sudo apt-get install gnupg

Once you have installed the tool, you should go ahead and create a key pair so as to begin encrypting your communications. This can be done by executing the following command:

gpg --gen-key

You will then be taken through a number of questions so that the keys can be configured. These questions include the following:

- Please select what kind of key you want: **(1) RSA and RSA (default)**

- What keysize do you want? **4096**

- Key is valid for? **0**

- Is this correct? **Y**

- Real name: **your name**

- Email address: name@address.com

- Comment: **comment to be available in your signature, optional**

- Change (N)ame, (C)omment, (E)mail or (O)kay/(Q)uit? **O**

- Enter passphrase: Provide a secure passphrase (should capture only upper and lower case, digits, symbols)

At this point, we can use entropy to generate the keys. This term is used for describing the degree of unpredictability that will be available in our system. This is used by GPG for the purpose of generating a random set of the GPG keys.

As this continues to run, open the terminal and then SSH into VPS. This is time for you to install the software you need, and do some other work as much as you can so that the generated entropy is much.

The Revocation Certificate

It is good for you to be in a position to invalidate the key pair since a security breach may occur, or maybe lose the secret key. The GPG software provides you with an easy way of doing this.

It is good for you to create the revocation key as early as you can, and then store it in a very secure place. The following command can be used for generating the key:

gpg --gen-revoke name@address.com

Once asked why you need to revoke, choose any of the available options.

To encrypt the message, you just have to use the "—encrypt" flag as shown below:

gpg --encrypt --sign --armor -r name@email.com file_name

To decrypt the message at the receiver's side, you have to execute the following command:

gpg file_name

To update the information regarding the key, execute the following command:

gpg --refresh-keys

Chapter 5- Hardware Configuration

Hard Disks Configuration

"fdisk" is a tool which can be used for an efficient partitioning of the hard disk in Linux. In Linux, only four primary partitions are allowed.

For you to use the fdisk utility, login as the root and then execute the command "fdisk *device."* It takes in the following commands:

- **p** -printing the partition table

- **n** -creating a new partition

- **d** -deleting a partition

- **q** -quitting without saving changes

- **w** -writing new partition table and exit

For the changes made to the disk to take effect, you have to execute the write (w) command.

To view all the available partitions in your system, execute the following command:

fdisk –l

To view a specific disk partition, such as "/dev/sda," execute the following command:

fdisk -l /dev/sda

For you to view the available fdisk commands, you have to mention a disk name as shown below:

fdisk /dev/sda

You can then type "m," and the commands will be presented to you.

Sometimes, you may need to view the partition table for your hard disk. Just enter the command mode of one of the disks such as **"/dev/sda,"** and then execute the following command:

fdisk /dev/sda

You can then type "p" for print, and the partition table will be printed.

Sometimes, you may need to delete a specific partition for a certain hard disk. Enter into the command of the disk. The command given below demonstrates this:

fdisk /dev/sda

You can then enter "d" for deletion. You will then be prompted to enter the number of the partition that you need to delete. Suppose I enter 3. I will be in the process of deleting the partition "/dev/sda3." You can then type "w" to write the changes to the partition table. The changes made will only take effect once you have rebooted the system.

Creating a New Partition

You may have left some empty space in the partition "/dev/sda," and you now need to partition it. Enter into the command mode in the disk by executing the following command:

fdisk /dev/sda

Type "n" for a new partition. To create an extended partition, press "e" and press "p" for a primary partition.

You can then enter the size of the new cylinder. For the case of the last cylinder, enter "+5000M." Once the partition has been created, do not forget to type "w" for writing and saving the changes, otherwise, it will not work.

It is good for you to format the new partition using the "mkfs" command. Use the following command:

mkfs.ext3 /dev/sda3

Configuring Network Interface Card

Most computers, and especially the server ones, come with two network interface cards built-into the motherboard. If you have additional cards, you can add them to the PCI expansion slots.

You can execute the command "lspci –vv" to check whether the card has been detected properly, and determine the kernel which has been assigned to it.

To be more specific, execute the command:

lspci -vv | grep Ethernet

Configuring a New Card

The tools used for network configuration are different in different Linux distributions. The following commands can be used for the sake of starting and stopping networking:

- sudo /etc/init.d/networking start

- sudo /etc/init.d/networking stop

- sudo /etc/init.d/networking restart

In Ubuntu, we use the "/usr/bin/gnome-nettool" tool for network configuration. If you have not installed this tool, use the command "apt-getinstall gnome-nettool" to install it.

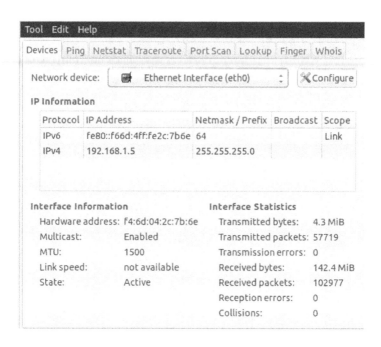

In Ubuntu, you can also choose to add the entries directly to the configuration file. This is the file "/etc/network/interfaces."

Dynamic IP:

...
...
auto eth1
iface eth1 inet dhcp

Static IP:

...
...
auto eth1
iface eth1 inet static
address 192.168.1.3
netmask 255.255.255.0
network 192.168.1.0
broadcast 192.168.1.254

You have to provide the address and the mask, but the system can calculate the rest of the values on your behalf. Configuration of DNS can be done in the file "/etc/resolv.conf."

In Red Hat/ Fedora, the console-based network configuration tool is the best for adding network devices. This is the tool "system-config-network."

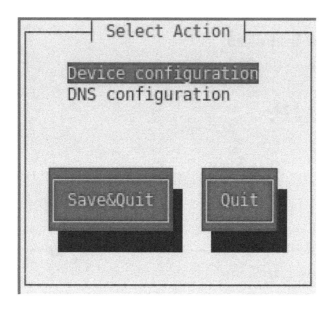

If you are adding a new network device, select the option for "New Device":

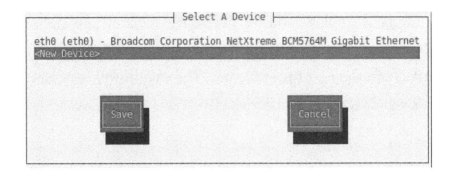

You can then select the kind of device that you need to add:

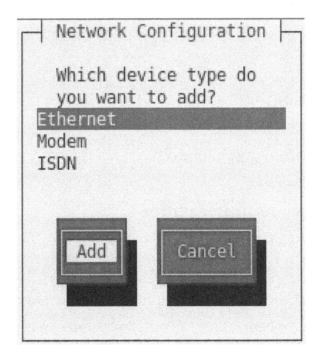

In the next window, add the necessary dynamic and static IP addresses. If you don't need to use these, go to the line for DHCP and then hit the space bar. The option will be selected. This is indicated by an asterisk (*).

Once you are done with the configuration, the device should show up in the list of configured devices, "/sbin/ifconfig."

Once you have added a new Ethernet device, a new file, that is, *"/etc/sysconfig/network-scripts/ifcfg-eth1"* will be generated:

DEVICE=eth1
BOOTPROTO=static
NETMASK=255.255.255.0
TYPE=Ethernet
HWADDR=00:10:17:24:bf:77
IPADDR=192.168.1.2

If you need to seek an explanation on the parts given above, you can open the file *"/usr/share/doc/initscripts-*/sysconfig.txt."*

If you need to bring up the new Ethernet interface, use the command:

ifup eth1

To bring down the interface, use the following command:

ifdown eth1

Configuration of DNS can be done in the file *"/etc/resolv.conf."*

The Firmware

Firmware is a small piece of code which is added to a device so that it can function as expected. This means that it acts as a way of programming the hardware so that it work well in the device.

The maintenance of the firmware is done by the company which manufactures the hardware.

Initial Setup

Begin by ensuring that your firmware file is available in the system. If you don't have this, search for it from the web.

If you have the file, check to make sure that it is not empty by using the following command:

```
$ ls -l /lib/firmware/iwlwifi-5000-1.ucode
```

```
-rw-r--r-- 1 root root 345008 2009-11-30 06:29
/lib/firmware/iwlwifi-5000-1.ucode
```

The size of our file is the value which is listed immediately after the user and group owners, and the value should be a non-zero. It is good for you to find an md5 hash and then compare it to your file, so that you can be sure that the file is not corrupted in any way. If the file has been corrupted, you will get an error message from the driver which should state that the file was found to be invalid or it failed to upload.

Kernel Event

In the second step, we should have the kernel sending an event to our udev subsystem. There exists a tool which can help us to monitor the event messages. Starting with the driver being unloaded, execute the following command:

$ udevadm monitor --property

You can then load the driver, but be aware that in most cases, once you load the driver on its own, you will be requested for the firmware. In some cases, something will have to be done so that the firmware can be loaded.

After initiation of the firmware, you should have the following udev event:

UDEV [167452165.246834] add /devices/pci0000:00/0000:00:07.0/firmware/0000: 00:07.0 (firmware)

UDEV_LOG=3
ACTION=add
DEVPATH=/devices/pci0000:00/0000:00:07.0/firmware/0000:00:07.0

SUBSYSTEM=firmware
FIRMWARE=e100/d101m_ucode.bin
SEQNUM=1206

Udev sending information to the Kernel

Once the udev has seen the firmware request, it will decide on the method of processing it.

The udev event can be watched by turning on an extra logging. This can be done by executing the following command:

$ sudo udevadm control --log-priority debug

Once the udev execution has been debugged, the logging output should be returned to the normal level using the following command:

$ sudo udevadm control --log-priority err

If the udev executes the *"formware.sh"* script, any found errors should be shown in the file "/var/log/syslog." Any errors observed in this case may be as a result of the file formware.sh or maybe the kernel. In case you see the error below:

udev firmware loader misses sysfs directory

You should just open the kernel bug. In case of any other error, you should just open the bug against udev.

Mounting and Unmounting Filesystems

Mount(8) is used for the purpose of mounting filesystems in Linux. It takes the following syntax:

mount *device mountpoint*

The command is associated with options, and some of these are discussed below:

- -a this mounts all the file systems in "**/etc**/fstab," except the ones which have been marked with "noauto," excluded by use of the −t flag, or the ones which have already been mounted.

- -d everything will be done except the real mount system call. It can be used with the −v flag for determination of what the mount (8) is intending to do.

- -f this forces an unclean file system to be mounted, or a write access to be revoked when downgrading the mount status of our file system from the read-write to read-only.

- -r the file system is mount to read-only. It is similar to the use of -o ro.

- -t fstype this will mount the file system type that you specify or mount file systems of a particular type only, it has a −a included.

- -u this is used for updating the options on our file system.

- -v this is for being verbose.

- -w this is for mounting the file system to be read-write.

unmount(8)

This is used for the purpose of unmounting a file system. This command will only take a single parameter, which can be either a mountpoint, the name of a device, or −a or −A.

If you need to force the unmounting to happen, you have to use the -of flag, and verbose, use −v flag. Remember that when you use the −A flag, there will be no attempt to unmount the root file system.

Chapter 6- Timing and Logging Services

The "date" command can be used for setting the time of the system. The implementation of this in GNU allows for different formats by which we can do this. Consider the examples given below:

To set the year only:

date -s 'next year'
date -s 'last year'

To set the month only:

date -s 'last month'
date -s 'next month'

To set the day only:

date -s 'next day'

```
date -s 'tomorrow'
date -s 'last day'
date -s 'yesterday'
date -s 'thursday'
```

If you need to set all of these at once, do it as follows:

```
date -s '2016-08-18 12:41:30'
```

The Hardware Time

After you have set the system time, sometimes, you may need to keep it in sync with the hardware clock. If you need to view the hardware time, you use the "—show." This is shown below:

hwclock —show

The hardware clock can also be set to the current system time. This is shown below:

hwclock —systohc

If you need to set the system time to the hardware time, then do it as follows:

hwclock —hctosys

To change the date, you have to use the "date" command. However, you have to enter the full format for the date. This is demonstrated below:

```
# date -s "20160817 08:25"
Tue Aug 16 08:30:00 BST 2016
```

Logging

In Linux, log files are located in "/var/log" by default. To see the list of directories which are stored in that directory, you just have to use the following command:

ls -l /var/log

You will find some log files in that directory. However, the contents of these files cannot be viewed directly by use of the "*cat*" command.

Suppose you have your Linux server and you need to view the user who is currently logged in. This can be done by use of the "who" command. If you are using CentOS or Debian, then this command will get the contents of the file "/var/run/utmp," but for Ubuntu users, it will read the contents of the file "/run/utmp."

In CentOS, you just have to open the terminal and type the command "who."

Create and Test Log Messages

We need to demonstrate how one can create their own log files. This should be done in the "/etc/rsyslog.conf" file. The contents of this file can be viewed in the vi editor by use of the following command:

vi /etc/rsyslog.conf

You should restart the service so as to load the config file:

/etc/init.d/rsyslog restart

You can the logger app so as to write your log message:

logger -p local4.info " This is a info message from local 4"

You can then open the file and you will find that this message was written:

cat /var/log/local4info.log

Rotation of the Log Files

Log files usually get bigger as more data is written to them. This can cause a problem with performance.

In Linux, log files are rotated but not deleted. During the rotation of a log, a new log file is created, the old log file is renamed and then compressed.

The rotation of the log files is usually done via the "logrotate" utility.

The Configuration File

The rotation of the logs relies on a configuration file named "*logrotate.conf.*" The file can be found under the directory "under /etc."

To view its contents, just open the terminal and execute the cat command as shown below:

cat /etc/logrotate.conf

In my case, I get the following:

 # see "man logrotate" for details
 # rotate log files weekly
weekly

 # keep 4 weeks worth of backlogs
rotate 4

 # create new (empty) log files after rotating old ones
create

```
# uncomment this if you want your log files
compressed
#compress

# packages drop log rotation information into this
directory
include /etc/logrotate.d

# no packages own wtmp, or btmp -- we'll rotate them
here
/var/log/wtmp {
    missingok
    monthly
    create 0664 root utmp
    rotate 1
}

/var/log/btmp {
    missingok
    monthly
    create 0660 root utmp
    rotate 1
}

# system-specific logs may be configured here
```

As you can see, it is not hard for you to understand the details of the above configuration file. The default setting is that the log files should be rotated on a weekly basis, and at least four back logs have to be maintained online. After the running of a program, a new log file is created, while the old one has to be compressed.

However, an exception exists for the btmp and wtmp files. The wtmp is responsible for keeping track of the system logins while the btmp is responsible for keeping track of any bad attempts to login. Such files are usually rotated on a monthly basis, and in case the previous btmp and wtmp files are found, then you will get no error.

The directory "etc/logrotate.d" is responsible for keeping the custom configurations for the log rotation. This directory can be viewed as follows:

etc/logrotate.d

You can run the logrotate manually, in which case one or more log files will be recycled. Consider the command given below:

ls -l /var/log

The command will give you the log files located in the "/var/log" directory. To force a rotation of the logs, execute the following command:

logrotate -fv /etc/logrotate.conf

Conclusion

We have come to the conclusion of this guide. The topics which are tested in the CompTIA Linux+ exam have been discussed, with the emphasis being on LX0-103 and LX0-104. The process of installing Linux is easy, and it can be done using a number of installation media. Each form of installation is associated with its own merits and demerits, so choose the best one according to what you need. The most popular form of installation of Linux is by use of a CD-ROM.

However, your computer should be capable of booting from the disk for this to work. The installation part is mostly tested in the CompTIA Linux+ exam, so it will be good for you to master its basics. The security of Linux systems is also greatly tested in CompTIA Linux+ exam. You should be aware of the various measures for securing Linux systems. Examples of these mechanisms include the use of firewalls, file permissions, GPG, and ensuring that the Linux kernel has been well secured. The process of configuring the various hardware tools has been discussed in detail, and this is an essential part in the CompTIA Linux+ exam. The various tools provided by the Linux command line are highly tested in the

CompTIA Linux+ exam, so there is a need for you to grasp the most important concepts regarding this.

www.ingramcontent.com/pod-product-compliance
Lightning Source LLC
LaVergne TN
LVHW052306060326
832902LV00021B/3736